DISCOVERING
YOUR DIVINE
FINGERPRINT

THE FORCE THAT MAKES **YOU** UNSTOPPABLE

Requests for information should be addressed to:
Elevate Life Publishing
8500 Teel Parkway
Frisco, TX, 75034
214-387-9833
http://elevatelife.com

Cover Design: www.theeastcogroup.com
Book Layout/Design: Elevate Life Publishing

Printed in Canada

TABLE OF CONTENTS

YOUR DEFINING MOMENTS   1

YOUR X FACTOR   13

YOUR 1%   25

YOUR THINK, BE, DO   35

YOUR LEADERSHIP   45

YOUR T-N-T   65

YOUR HABIT FORCE   81

YOUR UNSTOPPABLE FORCE   103

INTRODUCTION

A Message from Keith Craft

The key to all your future success and achievement is at the tip of your fingers, in your unique, God-given fingerprint – *Your Divine Fingerprint*. I am honored and pleased you have chosen to join me on this journey to reach your full, God-given greatness.

At the age of fourteen, I realized I had a fingerprint that nobody else had and or ever would have. In that moment, it became clear to me that God made me unique – just like He made you unique too!

> *"You have a fingerprint that no one else has to leave an imprint that no one else can leave!"*
> – Your Divine Fingerprint, p. 10

According to science, 99% of your DNA sequence is the same as every other persons DNA. So while science proves how similar we are, it also reveals how unique we are. *There is a crucial difference – a 1% difference – between you and every other person that has ever been – and ever will be – born.* Your 1% difference, revealed through your one-of-a-kind fingerprint, is a deposit of God's glory that makes you great!

> *"That which makes you different, makes you great!"*
> – Your Divine Fingerprint

You can be great in every area of your life. You can live a life of excellence and become an unstoppable force! You can live a life that leaves a legacy pointing to God. The good news is you do not have to create your greatness – you just have to unleash what God has already instilled in you!

My hope is, as I share my story about what God has done in my life, you will see the deposit of glory God gave you. I believe that this deposit is unique to you. It is up to you to discover, develop, and deploy this deposit to leave a legacy that points to Him. God desires to show you the power He has given you!

My prayer is simple. I pray that through this study you will be inspired to reach you full God-given greatness ... so that through you, others can see the greatness of God!

The Study Guide

This study guide provides a natural link between the book, "*Your Divine Fingerprint*", and the CD/DVD teaching sessions. The study guide, book, and CDs/DVDs are a set of complementary tools – working together synergistically to create a robust experience for self-study and small groups.

Please make sure you have these tools (CDs/DVDs, study guide, and book) as you lead yourself or others through this study. Each of the following eight chapters corresponds to a CD/DVD session and a chapter(s) from my book, *Your Divine Fingerprint*. They also include insightful quotes, supplemental content, key scriptures, and thought-provoking questions. At the end of each chapter is what we call *"Deploying Your Fingerprint."* It acts as the chapter capstone, helping you absorb, retain, and apply information you just learned by posing additional thought-provoking questions, outlining suggested action steps, and providing a notes/journal page to capture key takeaways.

Suggestions for Study Times

1. <u>Keep it simple.</u> Develop a plan (sample below) and pace yourself.

2. Stay consistent. Always open and close your study time with prayer. Commit to the time and place where you choose to study and remain consistent. Don't quit.
3. Expect results. Be honest and transparent with yourself and God as you answer the questions.

Sample Plan – Self Study

Begin with the study guide. Determine the related chapter(s) in the book, *Your Divine Fingerprint* and CD/DVD sessions.

- Read the chapter(s) in book (30 to 60 minutes).
- Listen to or watch the related CD/DVD session (30 minutes).
- Complete the respective chapter in the study guide (30 minutes).

Sample Plan – Leaders of a Group Study

Before the first meeting, ask the participants to purchase their materials and read the first chapter of the book. At your first meeting, you will show the DVD and then work through the study guide together. Before departing, encourage participants to reflect on the questions again before the next meeting. Also, have them read the book chapter(s) related to the group meeting.

The weekly reading will take about 30 to 60 minutes. This amount of reading may be new and/or challenging to some participants. Encourage them to break it into 10-minute, daily, bite size segments.

Triads

As you read *Your Divine Fingerprint*, watch the DVD teachings, and dive into this Study Guide, you will find that I often refer to triads (or triangles). I use triads as systematic teaching tools. In the Greek language, the symbol for a triangle is Delta. Delta literally means balance – it represents things that are congruent and things that work together. My systematic teaching method using triads helps people to connect-the-dots to things that work together – the elements of leadership patterns and principles that matter most.

I drew my first triad when I was 15 years old. I drew it to illustrate for my girlfriend, now wife, a philosophy of how relationships work. I took out a piece of paper and drew a triangle. On the left hand side I wrote her name. On the right side, I wrote my name. At the top, I wrote God. I said, "This is how I believe our relationship will work best – as long as we choose to be in relationship with each other. If you will be your best for God" – I drew an arrow from her name pointing up to God's name – "and I will be my best for God" – I drew an arrow up from my name to God's name – "we will meet at the top." I explained, "It's not so much about you and me as it is about "US" and Him! I believe great relationships are built by individuals who put God first." It was at that point I drew another arrow

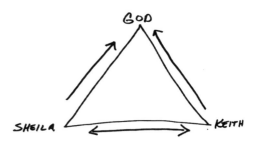

between our names. I said again, "If we are both our best for God, we will be our best for each other. Our common denominator is that both of us want what God wants for us." I then asked her if that was something that she agreed with and she said, "Yes!"

Since then, I have developed a number of triads. They remain the primary way I coach people in a process of personal growth and development. You will find triads at the end of each chapter of this Study Guide. They provide you with the specific roadmap to "Discover, Develop, and Deploy" your unique fingerprint – your unique 1%. As you follow this process, I believe you will discover, develop, and deploy your uniqueness, becoming all of "what" and "who" God intends you to become – an Unstoppable Force!

I look forward to hearing about the great things God does in your life!

God Bless You,
Keith Craft

"Not all moments are wonderful things, but every moment can be a supernatural event."

—Your Divine Fingerprint, p.6

1 YOUR DEFINING MOMENTS

Please reference Chapter 1 in the book, Your Divine Fingerprint and Session 1 of the DVD teaching series.

You have a fingerprint that is unique to you. Hidden inside your fingerprint is the deposit of greatness God has given you – and it is unique to you! The first thing you have to understand about the power of your fingerprint is the power found within the moments of our daily lives.

Moments happen every day. Some are defining moments, while others seem to slip by without a thought. Everybody has had more than one defining moment in his/her life. These moments, whether good or bad, positive or negative, healthy or unhealthy, all became defining moments when you decided to allow something in those moments to define you.

While reading the first chapter of *Your Divine Fingerprint* and watching the DVD, you likely thought about some defining moments in your life. They may have been associated with a graduation, marriage, birth, divorce, new business, death, a bankruptcy, or some other event.

Defining moments are not just "defining" in the moment itself, but also well beyond, as defining moments set a course for your future.

> *"The decisions you make today will not just affect your tomorrow but will determine your future."*
> *– Your Divine Fingerprint, p.2*

Reflect on some defining moments in your life. What is it about each that made it a defining moment for you?

_____

_____

_____

Think about each defining moment above and whether it has had a positive or negative impact on your life. In your mind, what made each either positive or negative?

_____

_____

_____

How do you define your moments so that your moments do not define you? You "Make Your Moments," "Momentum Your Moments," and "Miracle Your Moments" – a section follows for each of these.

——————— MAKE YOUR MOMENTS ———————

> "Moments are defined every time we make a decision, and our decision to define the moment is what gives power to the moment."
>
> – Your Divine Fingerprint, p. 2

When a defining moment comes along, you decide to either define the moment or allow the moment to define you. Although any given moment may seem powerful, there is always something much more powerful than any moment – how you choose to respond to that moment. **Your decision to define the moment empowers the moment.**

You have the power to define any moment you have experienced, will experience, or are experiencing. So, how do you define your moments? You make your moments. How do you make your moments? By making a choice to call on God.

Read John 2:1-11

Weddings, like the Wedding at Cana, had marital feasts that lasted up to seven days. One of the most important things about weddings, beyond the significance of two people committing their lives to one another, was the wine. Wine, when referenced in scripture, often represents joy, or a joyful occasion. When Mary told Jesus they had run out of wine, she was not just talking about the wine in the physical sense. Rather, she was saying, "We have run out of joy."

> "We cannot determine everything that happens to us, but we can define how what happens to us affects us."
> – Your Divine Fingerprint, p.6

Has there been a moment in your life when you were supposed to have had a great time and it ended up being the opposite? Describe it.

_____

_____

_____

_____

Many people "run out of wine" because they have allowed moments to define them instead of choosing to define the moment. They run out of joy and are left feeling empty and broken. A moment in time that was supposed to be joyful was actually joyless.

"Moments that define you can either confine you or refine you ... it's your choice."

The fact is, Mary decided to make the moment rather than allowing the moment to make her. Her decision defined the moment and gave it power!

Romans 8:28
"And we know that all things work together for good for those who love God, and who are called according to His purpose."

———— MOMENTUM YOUR MOMENTS ————

You begin to define your moments when you make a decision to turn them into momentum so you can move forward like never before. When you choose to see the positive in the negative, you create momentum in the moment. When you choose to learn from your experiences both good and bad, you create momentum. When you choose to be an energy producer and not an energy demander, you create momentum in any moment. When you understand that your attitude is the hinge upon which the door of your destiny swings, you can create momentum in any moment to open any door!

"You turn moments into momentum when you choose to seize the opportunity to take whatever has happened in your life and use it for your good."

– Your Divine Fingerprint p.6

In John 2:8, Jesus told the servants to get wastewater and give some to the master of the feast. How do you think the servants felt in this moment? Oftentimes, we do not turn our moments into momentum because we are too concerned with how we think something is going to make us look to others.

Has there been a time in life where you were scared to move forward with something because of how you thought it would be perceived? Describe it here.

_____

_____

_____

The servants filled the pots with dirty water, and Jesus took the dirty water and transformed it into wine. That's how it's supposed to be when we "momentum our moments." We take something that we do not feel is "good enough" – something we think is the waste at the end of the feast – and God makes it into the best.

God wants to show up for you in the midst of your moment. When you decide to bring to Him what you have, instead of thinking about how it will make you look, God can take your "waste" and turn it into "wine."

Isaiah 61:3
"...he will give a crown of beauty for ashes, a joyous blessing instead of mourning, festive praise instead of despair."

Do not let your moments overpower you; God gives us the power to define them.

──── MIRACLE YOUR MOMENTS ────

Miracles do not just happen, but moments do. When you take natural moments, negative or positive, and use them to create positive momentum, the moment becomes a super-natural moment – a miracle. When you use your power to decide how a moment will affect you, you can then begin to define the moment instead of the moment defining you. It is at this point that moment + momentum = miracle. You have the power to turn moments into miracles!

In John 2:7, the servants did a key thing that defined the moment as a miracle moment. They filled the water pots up to the brim. What does that say to us? Fill up your life to the brim! Don't just go to work, go to work and fill it up to the brim! Don't just have a family, fill your family up to the brim! Obey God like never before, and He will take every moment – your best and your worst – and turn them into miracles.

It is our responsibility to obey God and believe 100%, regardless of what is happening in our moments. We have to do our part. Give your best to your family, business, and relationships and let God worry about your worst.

It does not matter what the defining moments have been in your life. When God gets involved in the process, He takes your moments, and those moments become miracle moments.

Redefine your defining moments ... take the moments you listed at the beginning of this study and reevaluate

them based on how you want them to be defined.

_____

_____

_____

What do you need to start doing now in order to begin defining your moments?

_____

_____

_____

What do you need to stop doing now in order to begin defining your moments?

_____

_____

_____

My encouragement to you as you continue through this study is to BELIEVE! Believe you are special. Believe you have Greatness! Believe that God has a plan for your life and that He gave you your unique fingerprint for a reason. Believe you have incredible God-given value to bring everywhere you go, and begin bringing it NOW!

"You have the power to turn moments into miracles. Rather than having defining moments, we have miracle moments that define a super-natural life, and we can overcome all natural limitations and deficiencies."

– Your Devine Fingerprint p.7

DEPLOYING YOUR FINGERPRINT

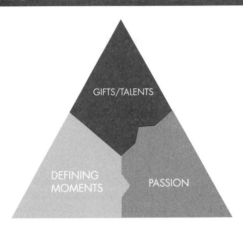

As a part of the THINK, BE, DO process, this guide is the beginning of your journey to discover, develop, and deploy your greatness to the world. After reading chapter 1 of *Your Divine Fingerprint*, watching the DVD teaching, and working through chapter 1 of this guide, answer the following questions.

DISCOVER YOUR DEFINING MOMENTS

Revisit your list of defining moments. As you reflect on these moments, what are some things you feel have shaped you into the person you are today?

_____

_____

_____

_____

_____

_____

What do you do well? Write down things you believe you have a talent or gift in.

_____

_____

_____

_____

DEVELOP YOUR PASSION

Based on your defining moments, what has shaped your passion? Why?

_____

_____

_____

_____

How can you begin to develop your gifts and talents to be utilized in a greater way?

_____

_____

_____

_____

DEPLOY YOUR GIFTS/TALENTS

- Begin to develop your gifts and talents.

- Find a mentor who can guide you in this process.

Notes:

Notes:

*"...the answer is not just within reach,
it is within YOU!"*

—*Your Divine Fingerprint, p. 19*

2 YOUR X FACTOR

Please reference Chapter 2 in the book, Your Divine Fingerprint and Session 2 of the DVD teaching series.

Everybody has a name – yet, few know who they really are. Everybody wants to succeed – yet, few have taken the time to define what personal success looks like. Everybody has an X Factor for success – yet, few discover, develop, and deploy it, so they never reach their full, God-given potential.

> *The truth is most people get more in life of what they do not want rather than what they do want because they never really decide what it is that they want.*
> *– Your Divine Fingerprint, p.20*

What does success look like to you?

_____

_____

_____

Do you believe you are experiencing it?

_____

_____

_____

MISCONCEPTION LEADS TO PRECONCEPTION

Most people live reactionary lives. They drift through life haphazardly, taking whatever life throws at them. As such, the world around them shapes how they see themselves and how they define success. The image they have of themselves may stem from their ethnicity or the era of history in which they were born, whether they are rich or poor, previous successes or failures, eye or hair color, where they are from, or any number of other personal distinctions. Misconceptions are born out of how they see themselves and what they believe about themselves.

Limited knowledge also leads to misconceptions. Everyone has limited knowledge about themselves and the world around them. Revisit the story of Ali Hafed on page 17 of *Your Divine Fingerprint*. Ali Hafed did not know he already had diamonds, so he sold his farm and spent the rest of his life looking for them elsewhere. His story is an example of how limited knowledge affected the impact he made on the world.

Both the world around us and our limited knowledge shape the beliefs we have about ourselves. These beliefs give birth to misconceptions we have about ourselves that lead to preconceptions we each have about the people, places, and things around us. In other words, what we preconceive about people, places, and things is a result of how we perceive ourselves.

We do not see people, places, and things how they are – we see them through the lens of how **we** are. For example, if you look at a lemon through a pair of sunglasses having blue lenses, what color is the lemon? It is green, right? No! The lemon is yellow. The color of the lemon does not change; rather, what changes is how you see the lemon.

Preconceptions keep us from achieving success to the level we can, because we do not have the knowledge of how special, unique, and wonderful we really are.

Genesis 1:27-28
27 So God created man in His own image; in the image of God He created him; male and female He created them. 28 Then God blessed them, and God said to them, "Be fruitful and multiply; fill the earth and subdue it; have dominion over the fish of the sea, over the birds of the air, and over every living thing that moves on the earth."

God created you in His image, according to His likeness, and blessed you to be fruitful, multiply, rule over, and subdue the things of the earth. He created you to succeed, to be a champion. People who view themselves as God sees them generally feel good about themselves. They know He loves them and has a plan for them. When they lose sight of being created in the image of God, their self-image becomes distorted. They find the world over which God created them to rule and subdue, ruling and subduing them.

Does your self-image line up with who God says you are? This is an important question as our perception of where we are in life right now may be more important than where we actually are! When we take a step back and view ourselves the way God sees us, our life starts to look a lot more like God intended it to.

What do you think success looks like to God?

_____

_____

_____

X FACTOR DEFINED

You have an X Factor for success, everybody does. An X Factor is, "The element or elements that are vital to an observable change or result." In other words, all things being equal, if you just add an "X" to an equation, process, or strategy, X will produce a result not possible in any other way.

Most people never realize they have an X Factor for success. Your realization begins with you knowing that God created us in His image. He gave each of us a one-of-a-kind fingerprint, natural evidence that we each have something in us that nobody else has – a unique deposit of God's glory. This deposit of glory is your X Factor for success. It is up to you to discover, develop, and deploy it so that you can leave an imprint on this world like no other for His glory. In doing so, you reflect the image of God and your X Factor for success produces results in your life not possible in any other way.

BELIEVING IS SEEING

Read Mark 8:10-26

You can't see what you don't believe. You can only see what you choose to believe.

The Pharisees in this story, despite already watching Jesus earlier in this chapter feed 4,000 men plus women and children, asked for a sign. They asked to see what they already did not believe and Jesus denied their request.

Shortly thereafter, a blind man was brought to Jesus. The friends that led him to Jesus chose to believe that He could restore the blind man's vision – they had faith.

Do the people around you have this kind of faith? When you don't see something for yourself, do you have people who can believe with you and for you? Who are they?

_____

_____

_____

Jesus put His DNA and His fingerprint on the blind man. In doing so, He changed the blind man's life forever. God gives us His DNA to not just heal us or make us unique, but to reflect Him.

To experience God's definition of success in our lives and the lives of our families, we have to believe that He created us for success. He wants us to experience it – not just according to the world's definition of success but according to His definition of success. It should add value both personally and professionally. Success is not about money. Rather, it is about:
- discovering your uniqueness
- developing your gifts and talents, competencies, and vision

- deploying your capacity to develop yourself, your dreams, beliefs, and willingness to take action to reach your full God-given potential

How do you add value right now to:

- Your Church _____

- Your Family _____

- Your Job _____

- Your Friends _____

Success begins and ends with your belief.

"Whatever the mind of a man can conceive and believe, it can achieve."
-Napoleon Hill

If you can see it and believe it, then with God's help, it is within your reach!

Where is your belief currently? How do you need to believe in order to be where you feel like God wants you to be?

_____
_____
_____
_____

DEPLOYING YOUR X FACTOR

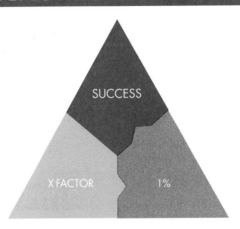

After reading this study, watching the teaching, and reading chapter 2 of *Your Divine Fingerprint*; take a moment to consider these questions:

DISCOVER YOUR X FACTOR

How do you define success?

_____

_____

_____

What has been the X Factor in your past that has produced success in your life?

_____

_____

What is your big dream?

_____

_____

_____

DEVELOP YOUR 1%

What do you feel is the next step to living your dreams?

_____

_____

_____

What are three important things you can do to begin your journey to success?

_____

_____

_____

Where can you add value that you are not adding now?

_____

_____

_____

DEPLOY YOUR SUCCESS

- Begin to implement the steps listed above. Once you have completed that, take more steps.

- Think of, and apply one idea to move you to your next level.

- Take one action step, no matter how great or small towards your big dream.

Notes:

_____

_____

_____

_____

_____

_____

_____

_____

_____

_____

_____

_____

_____

_____

_____

_____

_____

_____

_____

_____

_____

_____

_____

_____

_____

_____

_____

Notes:

_____

_____

_____

_____

_____

_____

_____

_____

_____

_____

_____

_____

_____

_____

_____

_____

_____

_____

_____

_____

_____

_____

_____

_____

_____

_____

_____

_____

"Your unique fingerprint is what will give you the power to leave an imprint on people, places, and things that you come in contact with. God gave you your fingerprint so that you could exemplify GREATNESS!"

—Your Divine Fingerprint, p.37

3 YOUR 1%

Please reference Chapter 3 in the book, Your Divine Fingerprint and Session 3 of the DVD teaching series.

Look at your hand. Notice your fingerprint. There has never been, nor will there ever be, another person who has your fingerprint. In years past, people's fingerprints were a primary identifier of their involvement in crimes and accidents, whether victims or culprits. However, I believe God gave you your fingerprint for a different and much greater purpose – to exemplify the greatness He has deposited in you!

YOUR 1% DIFFERENCE

Researchers say that 99% of all human DNA is the same. While science proves how similar we all are in our DNA, it also reveals how unique we are. In fact, it reveals a crucial difference – a 1% difference – that exists between you and every person who ever has been, and will be, born.

> *"Your 1% difference is a deposit of God's glory that makes you great!"*
> *– Your Divine Fingerprint, p.35*

Your fingerprint is an outward representation of your unique 1% - the part of you that is different from everybody else.

What are some ways you know you are unique and different from others?

_____

_____

_____

God created you with your 1% in mind. He gave you your fingerprint to leave an imprint that nobody else can leave.

There are two important things to understand before you can fully grasp this:

- You are fearfully and wonderfully made. (Psalm 139:14)

- You are created in the image and likeness of God. (Genesis 1:26)

You are not who you think you are. You are not who other people think you are. You are not even who you think others think you are. You are who God says you are!

YOUR FINGERPRINT

> God gave you a unique fingerprint to leave an imprint that no one else can leave.
>
> – Your Divine Fingerprint, p. 8

You are unique – not just on the outside but also on the inside. God has given you unique dreams, visions and plans, and has given you a unique calling to accompany them. Your 1% is a representation of all of these things. The 1% that is inside of you will determine what comes out of you and what comes out of you will determine the world around you.

How does your world appear to you right now?

_____

_____

_____

Do you feel like it is a result of yourself or other people/ circumstances?

_____

_____

_____

Despite all of this, the 99% of you that is similar to everybody else can keep you the same as everybody else, if allowed to. However, you can overcome your 99% (your similarity to everybody else) by leading yourself to develop your 1%. In other words, the unique part of you must lead the ordinary part of you in order for you to leave the imprint of your greatness in the world.

> _"Life is not what happens to us, but what we make happen through us."_
>
> _- Your Divine Fingerprint, p.35_

Read Luke 7:36-50

Seeing a person or a situation the same way that everyone else sees them will cause you to overlook the greatness they could potentially bring to your life. God has put them in your presence and regardless of who you think they are, they have something to bring to your life.

Jesus told a story to reframe Simon's thoughts – shifting them from what he perceived was happening and who he believed people to be – to what was really happening.

When we cannot see past our 99% – the part of us that is like everyone else and only sees what everybody else sees, thinks what everybody else thinks, and leads us to believe what everybody else believes – we miss God at work. We find ourselves wondering, "Where is God?"

Our 1% sees past our 99% and allows us to see God at work in ALL things. In this story, Jesus uses His 1% to help Simon see past his 99%.

If we see past the 99% of ourselves and see what the 1% sees, then we will develop our 1%.

God wants us to bring our 1% to every situation, every day. Why? Because to Him, this is the best part of who we are. When we do this, our 1% truly leads the 99% in us that causes us to miss the mark. Our 1% is the God part of us that is meant to reflect Him, and when we honor Him with it we truly begin to walk in the greatness He meant for us!

Think of a time when you looked at someone or some situation through the lens of your 99%. Next time, how

can you see them through your 1%?

_____

_____

_____

—————— YOUR 99% VERSUS YOUR 1% ——————

Let's compare what the 99% of you sees versus the 1% that the God in you is supposed to see. Underneath each one of these is a self-talk that we can sometimes talk ourselves into believing. Take the opportunity below to make some notes about your self-talk.

99% Sees – Failure "My past negative outcomes will be perpetuated if I try again."	**1% Sees - Fortune** "My failures are filled with a fortune of lessons. With God's guidance, my failures will become my fortune." "The only man who never makes a mistake is the man who never does anything." —Theodore Roosevelt
99% Sees - Fear "I'd rather not risk others seeing me fail." "I'd rather not try than have to live with myself if I did fail."	**1% Sees - Faith** "God has not given me a spirit of fear. Therefore when I feel like fear is stopping me from reaching success I don't just fake it until I make it; I FAITH it until I make it!"

99% Sees - Familiar "Family of Origin. Blood is thicker than water. My family is all I've seen, all I've been told, and all I know. I can't change my family, or the issues I have with them." "I am limited by the beliefs of those I choose to do life with."	**1% Sees - Family of Choice** "I can choose to surround myself with those that believe what I believe so that together our beliefs can flourish."
99% Sees – Falsehood "Lies have been spoken over me, and I accept them as the truth about myself."	**1% Sees - Fact** "I was created in the Image of God. He blessed me to be fruitful and multiply to subdue and have dominion over the world around me."

DEPLOYING YOUR 1%

"What you believe is more important than what anyone will ever tell you. What you believe about life, relationships, money, food, love, sex, exercise, food, pets, God, politics, business, heaven and hell, the economy, and last but not lease, YOURSELF will drive all your behaviors and the actions you take."
—Your Divine Fingerprint, p.30

<u>Four Forces that Determine your 1% Deployment</u>
1. Your capacity to develop yourself
2. Your ability to believe
3. Your ability to dream
4. Your willingness to take action

DISCOVER YOUR DIFFERENCE

What comes to mind when you think about what your 1% Factor is? Write down specifics.

_____

_____

_____

_____

What influences have shaped your life the most up to this point?

_____

_____

_____

_____

_____

DEVELOP YOUR FINGERPRINT

Define the specifics of what you think your finger-print represents. What is specifically unique about you?

_____

_____

_____

_____

DEPLOY YOUR IMPRINT

Be intentional about understanding and leaving your 1% imprint in your extended circle of influence.

Notes:

_____

_____

_____

_____

_____

_____

_____

_____

_____

_____

_____

_____

_____

_____

_____

_____

_____

_____

_____

_____

*"As a man thinks in his heart,
so is he."*

—Proverbs 23:7 NKJV

4 YOUR THINK, BE, DO

Please reference Chapter 4 and 5 in the book, Your Divine Finger-print and Session 4 of the DVD teaching series.

How we think, determines what is in our heart, or who we will be.

– Proverbs 4:23 NLT
"Above all else guard your heart, for it affects everything you do."

What is in our heart, or who we have chosen to Be, effects everything we Do. So if we are going to guard our hearts, then we will have to protect our hearts against the very thing that determines what enters into our heart – our own thinking!

Your thoughts are like a plane approaching an airport. Your mind is the control tower. The landing strip is your heart. As the plane (thought) begins to approach the air-port, the pilot radios the control tower (mind) and asks for permission to land. The controller (you) in the con-trol tower (your mind) says, "No!" The plane (thought) is not allowed to land (in your heart). The landing strip (your heart) does not decide if the plane lands. If it did, all of the planes would land. Or, said another way, all of your thoughts would land in your heart. The phrase "follow your heart" is wrong. You are supposed to lead your heart. Your mind (control tower) controls your heart/emotions (landing strip) – not the other way around!

Your thoughts (things you allow yourself to meditate on) ultimately determine who you are.

The pathway to the greatness that God has already put within you can be summed up in this equation:

THINK + BE + DO = HAVE

In other words, every situation that you see starts with the way you think about the situation. Then, based on the way you think about it, you develop an attitude and feelings about it, or a way of being. Then, you take action based on the way you think, and the way you feel about it. The way you choose to think, feel and act about any situation or circumstance in life will determine what you have from that situation.

If you do not like what you have from your current Think, Be, Do – whether it be the condition of a relationship, your career, a financial challenge, or something else – change will only happen if you **Think** differently.

Go in reverse order. List some things you Have, and trace them back to see how your Think, Be and Do led you to them.

_____

_____

_____

_____

What are some areas that you are aware of where you need to do some things differently? How can you Think, Be, and Do differently than you have in the past?

_____

_____

_____

_____

Many times, the only difference between successful and unsuccessful people is the way a successful person chooses to think about a situation. Unfortunately, most people don't make the connection between where they are in life and the way they think. They develop a philosophy of, "life just happens," "the hand they were dealt" or the "luck of the draw."

Most people live their lives this way – by default and not by design. God designed you. He created you to live not by default, by accident, or even happenstance but rather, to live by design.

What are some areas where you have allowed yourself to live on the "default" side of life?

_____

_____

_____

If you are going to design your life to have maximum value in what matters, then you first have to determine what matters most to you.

"How you Think ... Be ... Do in life, will determine what you will Have in life."

—Your Divine Fingerprint p. 49

Read Luke 4:1-14

THINK SPIRIT-LED

The things we allow to fill us (our thoughts, time), eventually lead us. In Luke 4:1, it says that Jesus was full of the Spirit. Being full of the Holy Spirit enabled Him to be led by the Holy Spirit. We have to decide what we are going to be full of, as whatever you are full of will eventually lead you.

What is something you are allowing or have allowed yourself to be "full of" that has ended up leading you?

_____

_____

_____

God's power empowers you when you pass the tests you face. Any temptation is a test of what is most important to you. Therefore, make important to you what is important to God and you will pass the "what matters most" test.

BE CORE-VALUES BASED

Your Core Values define what matters most to you. However, most people have not defined their Core Values, much less intentionally aligned them with what is important to God.

Revisit page 80 in *Your Divine Fingerprint*, specifically the triangle. This triangle is representative of the core values I had adopted at age 15. As Sheila and I talked, I first emphasized the importance of our individual relationships with God and then our relationship together. This established Relationship as my number one core value. By saying, "Let's be our best for God", I established Excellence as a core value for our relationship. By saying, "Let's always communicate", I established Communication as a Core Value. By saying, "Let's do our best to talk things out before we leave each other and go our separate ways for the day", I established Conflict Resolution as a Core Value.

Only you can decide what matters most to you.

Take a few moments and write down your top 3 Core Values.

_____

_____

_____

DO A MASTERPIECE

Please Read the Michelangelo story on page 49-50, and page 74 of *Your Divine Fingerprint*.

Our lives are similar to the marble that Michelangelo shaped into a masterpiece. Until we allow God to shape us, we will not become all that He ultimately created us to be – His masterpiece. This becomes possible when we value what God values. When we understand what matters most we can live a life that most matters. This allows God to bring His glory to us, shaping each of us into a masterpiece.

The enemy of your soul has been trying his best since the beginning of your life to keep you from understanding that you are God's son or daughter. God intentionally created you for a specific purpose. He did not intend for you to remain a piece of marble. He made you to become a masterpiece. He engineered you for greatness. He sent His son, Jesus, so that you would believe. If you will believe, you allow God to do something in you that you could never do on our own.

In reading this, you may have realized that what matters most is valuing what God values – in essence, having a relationship with Him and placing Him above all else in your life. Pray this simple prayer.

> *"Dear Heavenly Father,*
> *Thank you for loving me, thank you for creating me and giving me life. And now today I give my life back to you. I ask you, Jesus, to be Lord of my life, to be first in my life. Thank you for loving me, thank you for accepting me, thank you for forgiving my sins. I give you my life from this day forward. Amen.*

If you prayed this prayer for the first time, please visit my website keithcraft.org. We have some great tools to help you as you begin your walk with God.

DEPLOYING YOUR THINK, BE, DO

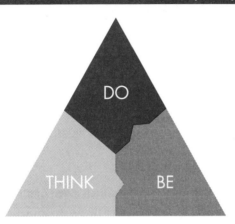

After reading this study, watching the teaching, and reading chapter 4-5 of *Your Divine Fingerprint*; take a moment to consider these questions:

DISCOVER YOUR THINK

Everything begins with a way of thinking. Think of a problem or situation you are facing right now. Ask yourself these questions:

1. How do I currently think about/perceive this problem?

2. How can I think differently/better about this problem? (Consider all the angles)

After considering your answers to these questions, ask yourself:

What can I do to ensure the possible solutions align with my core values?

_____

_____

_____

DEVELOP YOUR BE

It is important to realize that we cannot control what a person does to us or how a situation affects us, but we can always control how we respond.

Reflect on a time when you had a negative attitude toward a situation. How can you use your core values to choose a different response in the future?

_____

_____

_____

DEPLOY YOUR DO

- Take Action. Don't wait to feel better. Act your way into a feeling, don't feel your way into an action! Begin to act as if your feelings aren't hurt. Begin to actively seek win-win solutions to a problem or a business deal that has hit a wall.

- Encourage others. Even when you feel offended or hurt, find one positive thing about that person or situation.

_____
_____
_____
_____
_____
_____
_____
_____
_____
_____
_____
_____
_____
_____
_____
_____
_____
_____
_____
_____
_____
_____
_____
_____

"Leadership is the capacity of an individual to Discover their Passion, Develop their Vision, and Deploy their Greatness that elevates them personally and creates the ability to Empower others to do the same."

—Your Divine Fingerprint, p.101

5 YOUR LEADERSHIP

Please reference Chapter 6 in the book, Your Divine Fingerprint and Session 5 of the DVD teaching series.

The hardest and most important thing you will ever do is to lead yourself... beyond your normal... beyond your need to feel appreciated... beyond you!

Leadership is Always a Way of Thinking First, that Determines a Way of Being, that Becomes a Way of Doing.

The way you Think about God, yourself, and others will determine your Be, or how you are as a person. How you Be, your attitudes, beliefs, and self-image will determine how you Do, the decisions you make that ultimately make you. Ultimately, your Think, Be, and Do determine what you Have in life!

How you think about God will determine your whole philosophy of life. If you think God is real, then you can believe that you were born for a purpose. If you don't think God is real, your sense of purpose will be shaped by that belief. This is the foundational truth the rest of our beliefs will be based on. It will shape how we see EVERYTHING else.

How you think about yourself will shape your Being as it relates to your self-image and your self-esteem. How you think about others will determine your attitude toward them. Your attitude, which springs from your Being, will affect everyone and everything in your life.

Your attitude is the hinge upon which the door of your destiny swings. Your attitude is YOU! Who you are (BE) as a person, will manifest in your way of Doing life. Your attitude, your behaviors, and the actions you take all start with Your Thinking. Therefore, leadership begins with THINKING differently about God, yourself, and the world around you.

What is an action that you have taken recently that you can trace back to a thought that you had? Good or bad.

_____

_____

_____

Reflect on a time when you had negative thoughts about a person or a situation and it felt natural to you. How will you lead yourself to think better?

_____

_____

_____

> *"You know you're maturing, when you have a continual desire to Think...Be and Do better. It is God's unchanging will that we change for the better."*

DISCOVER YOUR PASSION

Leadership begins with Passion! Passion can be defined as an extravagant fondness, enthusiasm, or desire for anything. The fact is, once you discover your Passion you can begin to develop your Vision, which is the picture of the future you want. As you lead your Passion and Vision, you will deploy your Greatness. Which I call your 1% Factor – Your Unstoppable Force!

Often times our passion is revealed through the things we can be frustrated with. However, we have to separate a person or organization from a frustration and get to the root of what the passion is that is being expressed.

Have you identified an area of passion you can engage in on a new level? How will you lead yourself to develop this passion?

_____

_____

_____

_____

_____

_____

DEVELOP YOUR VISION

Vision is a God inspired portrait of a better future! In order to accomplish anything truly great in life we must embrace and develop a vision that calls the greatness out of us. A compelling vision compels you to be your best, stay in the fight when others would throw in the towel, and allows others in your life to join you as you pursue it. Your vision may be refined over time, but if you pursue it with your passion it moves you to step out as a leader and, in the end, leads to greatness.

What are some areas in your life where you have developed a passionate vision for what COULD be?

_____

_____

_____

DEPLOY YOUR LEADERSHIP

Leadership is Discovering That When You Change What Needs to Change for the Better IN You, You Gain the Power to Change What Is Around You.

When we learn to lead ourselves through change, we gain the confidence to believe that anything around us can change for the better. We won't see the kind of change we dream of or hope for until we embrace the fact that WE need to change! We often expect others to do FOR us what we aren't willing to do for ourselves or for others. We hope other people will change instead of accepting the uncomfortable truth that most often WE need to change if there can be any hope of things being different or changing for the better. Leaders learn to focus on what needs to change IN themselves before they hope to see change in those around them and yet, because leaders think this way, they have hope that those around them can change too. Best of all, when we embrace the fact that WE can change we gain the power to influence positive change in those around us.

In what an area of your life have you experienced frustration? Can you identify a potential change in you or

your behavior that would have an impact on the change you want to see in this area?

_____

_____

_____

_____

_____

_____

Leadership is the Art of Ruling Oneself – Spirit, Soul, and Body—and Doing What You Don't FEEL Like Doing, When It Needs to Be Done.

Proverbs 25:28 (NKJV)
"Whoever has no rule over his own spirit is like a city broken down, without walls."

Ruling your spirit is inside out living. It's a lifetime commitment to lead your mind (Think), your attitude (Be), and your body (Do) everyday based on your core values and what matters most to you rather than living by default based on what "feels good" right now. It is guarding your heart, governing your mind, and guiding your body based on who you want to be rather than what you want in a moment. It is relentless correction and redirection of your thinking every day.

Normal thinkers struggle with direction in life because they don't correct themselves enough. Leadership thinkers understand that if you will CORRECT YOURSELF when you know you need correction, you will have the discipline to DIRECT YOURSELF when you need direction.

"I am indeed a king because I know how to rule myself."
— Pietro Aretino

DO HARD THINGS!

When you do hard things you are training yourself to do GREAT things!

Doing hard things always begins with doing the little things. In faithfully doing the little things, even when no one is watching or can even see, we develop a personal spirit of excellence!

Discipline is the foundation of excellence! It is in the small, unheralded moments that we develop the personal capacity for true greatness.

What is a daily discipline you can embrace to grow your excellence? (Make your bed every day? Work out? Do the dishes before going to bed?)

_____

_____

_____

———— LEADERSHIP VS. NORMALSHIP ————

Having a "normal" thought process and a "leadership" thought process isn't dependent on a position or title within an organization. There are many people in leadership positions who think "normal" and there are many in normal positions who think "leadership." Both share something in common – neither will be in their current positions for long.

The person who thinks "leadership" and has an attitude of leadership will act like a leader and before long, they will be in a position of leadership. Ultimately, if you think like a leader, you will have the extraordinary in life.

Conversely, the person who thinks "normal" will have a common minded attitude and act in life no better than anyone around them. If you think normal, you will have what is ordinary.

The exercise below illustrates what it is to Think Leadership as opposed to thinking normally. Rank yourself by filling in a box to the left of center if your thinking tends to be more to the side of Leadership and to the right if your thinking tends to be more to the side of Normalship.

Leadership	Versus	Normalship
Live with a transcendent cause	□□□□□□□□□□	Live with a what's–in–it–for–me? attitude
Embrace resistance	□□□□□□□□□□	Resist resistance
Refuse to be offended	□□□□□□□□□□	Exercise your right to be offended
Do not gossip	□□□□□□□□□□	Gossip if it's true
Believe the best when the worst has been displayed	□□□□□□□□□□	Believe the worst especially if the worst has been displayed
Desire to be your best	□□□□□□□□□□	See no need to change
Lead yourself first	□□□□□□□□□□	Want others to change first
See what is possible	□□□□□□□□□□	See things as impossible

Leadership	Versus	Normalship
Act your way into a feeling	□□□□□□□□□□	Feel your way into an action
Do whatever it takes	□□□□□□□□□□	Do whatever is easiest
Do more than you are asked	□□□□□□□□□□	Do only what is required
Love people the way they need to be loved	□□□□□□□□□□	Love others the way you love
Give generously (above and beyond)	□□□□□□□□□□	Give obligatorily (what you have to)
Develop your personal greatness	□□□□□□□□□□	Despise the greatness in others
Practice like it's game time	□□□□□□□□□□	Practice like it's practice
Exhibit confidence	□□□□□□□□□□	Exhibit insecurity
Extend mercy	□□□□□□□□□□	Pronounce judgement
Seek to understand	□□□□□□□□□□	Seek to be understood
Overcome	□□□□□□□□□□	Overwhelm
Display a spirit of excellence	□□□□□□□□□□	Display a spirit of perfectionism
Pro-activate	□□□□□□□□□□	Procrastinate
Live Core Values	□□□□□□□□□□	Live for others' approval
Seek victory in adversity	□□□□□□□□□□	Become a victim of adversity
Focus on self-improvement	□□□□□□□□□□	Focus on self-pity
Forgive	□□□□□□□□□□	Resent
Find good	□□□□□□□□□□	Find faults
Have high expectations of yourself	□□□□□□□□□□	Have high expectations of others

THE TWO MOST IMPORTANT THINGS ABOUT LEADERSHIP

SELF-LEADERSHIP

Whatever area of life that you choose to lead yourself in, you create the capacity to grow and develop in that area. Fundamentally, if you cannot lead yourself, it is impossible to lead others.

Self-Leadership in any area might be the most difficult thing that you ever do; but it is also the most important thing that you will ever do.

What is an area of your life that you need to begin to lead yourself better?

_____

_____

_____

Self-Leadership builds: Self-Respect

Your insecurity will often be the thing that keeps you from respecting yourself. When you can't respect yourself, you will have a hard time respecting others.

One of the greatest things you can begin to understand about respect is that it is a gift you give. Often times you may feel that respect is to be earned, but when you can truly respect yourself, you will learn that respect is a gift that you have the power to give others.

The roadmap to Respect:

Faithfulness breeds trust.
Faithfulness is key to developing trust with another person. The more you decide to be loyal and dedicated to a person, the more you will foster trust between you.

Trust breeds intimacy
If trust is based on your ability to be faithful, your ability to be authentic (intimate) will be based on the amount of trust that you have with yourself or another person. The more intimate you are as a person, the more you are able to love. If you have the ability to be intimate, then you have the power to be real about what the problems are in yourself or a relationship. If you have the power to be real about a problem, you then have the power to solve the problem.

Intimacy breeds respect.
If you respect yourself, you have the power to be unoffendable. The root of your offense will stem from making another person's opinion of you of greater importance than how you see yourself. If you respect yourself, another person's opinion of you will not be more important than your respect for yourself.

Self-Leadership elevates your: Character

Your character is not what you say, or even what you do, it is ultimately who you are on the inside. Your heart can lead your intentions, but it is your character that will lead your actions. So often, people with great hearts have low character and no integrity. Why? ...because they do not lead themselves. Your level of character will determine your level of integrity. When you choose to lead yourself, you develop greater character. When you have great character, you are empowered to operate in integrity.

In what aspects of your character could you use improvement?

_____

_____

_____

_____

_____

_____

How can you lead yourself to elevate this aspect of your character?

_____

_____

_____

_____

_____

_____

Self-Leadership improves your: Confidence

When you are leading yourself it is okay to be confident. Confidence, not arrogance is one of the best side effects of leading yourself. As a matter of fact, self-confidence is a necessary step on the path to self-mastery. Self-Discovery leads to Self-Development. Self-Development leads to Self-Confidence. Self-Confidence leads to Self-Competence. Self-Competence in turn leads to Self-Mastery!

Confidence is knowing that it doesn't matter what today looks like, you are leading yourself into a better future.

Confidence is not considering yourself above another person, it is knowing that regardless of another person's attitude or actions towards you, you are going to be better tomorrow than you are today.

SERVANT-LEADERSHIP

Ultimately, Self-Leadership is not SELFISH leadership. It is not about being the best for your own benefit. Your self-leadership develops to the fullest when you serve others.

In one word, Servant Leadership is generosity.

You are generous when you focus on what you have to give, not what you want to receive.

As with most things, Servant-Leadership is a way of thinking. It is the desire to live with a transcendent cause. Most people live for today with little thought for the future, so how can you live with a transcendent mindset? By choosing to focus on what you have to give others. What you have to give is ultimately rooted in three key areas. This is called being T-Rated.

T-Rated:

Time

You can choose to serve others with your time. Giving up an hour or a few moments in service of your church or a charitable organization is a great way to get started with Servant-Leadership. Or, you can choose to be a Servant-Leader with the people closest to you by making important to you what is important to them and investing time into their interests.

Talent

You can choose at any time in your life to take your 1% and not just use it for your own benefit; but for the benefit of others. Think today of how you can take the unique fingerprint that God has given you and be generous towards another person with it.

Treasure

How can you Servant-Lead with your treasure? Money is a big deal to everyone. It's also a big deal to God. You can choose to store up treasures in heaven (Matthew 6:20) by being generous with your money.

When you choose to be generous in these three areas and focus on them with a heart to give and not receive, you are truly leading yourself to become not just a Self-Leader, but a Servant-Leader.

How can you grow your SELF- and SERVANT-leadership capacity?

_____

_____

_____

_____

You are generous when you focus on what you can do, not what you can't do.

Never allow yourself to say: "that's not my job."

Put your hand over your heart and repeat this:

- I will never say: "I'm not paid to do that."

- I can do all things through Christ who is my strength.

- If I'm in the room, no matter what the problem is, I'm a part of the solution, not a part of the problem.

How can you be a part of the solution right now in an area of your life?

_____

_____

_____

_____

_____

_____

_____

_____

Servant Leadership is your: Greatest Capacity Developer.

Another definition of leadership is: "Your capacity to personally grow and develop so that you are empowered to help others do the same."

Do you find fulfillment in helping others grow?

Whether you realize it or not, you are the key for another person's greatness to be launched into the world.

The more you focus on giving and not receiving, and the more you focus on doing what you can, not what you can't, the more you will develop your capacity. The more you develop your capacity, the more you will add value everywhere you go.

As you increase your ability to lead yourself, you will have the confidence to serve others, which will ultimately unleash your 1% to the world.

What is one thing you can do this week to serve another person?

_____

_____

_____

_____

DEPLOYING YOUR LEADERSHIP

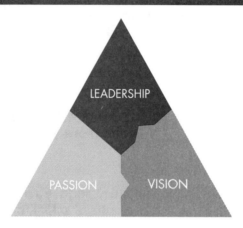

After reading this study, watching the teaching, and reading chapter 6 of *Your Divine Fingerprint;* take a moment to consider these questions:

What in your life can frustrate you at times? Understanding that frustration, how do you feel that can develop into a passion?

_____

_____

_____

_____

_____

_____

_____

_____

_____

_____

How can you lead your passion into a vision for your business or family?

_____

_____

_____

What part of your Normalship needs to be moved to Leadership? What are some little things that you need to do now that are hard for you?

_____

_____

_____

How are you going to implement Self-Leadership more in your life?

_____

_____

_____

What is harder for you: faithfulness, trust, intimacy or respect?

_____

_____

_____

How are you determining to grow in your ability to lead yourself?

_____

_____

_____

_____

_____

What part of Servant-Leadership do you need to focus on the most?

_____

_____

_____

_____

_____

Who is the greatest Servant-Leader you know? What makes them a great Servant-Leader? What can you learn from your chosen Servant-Leader and implement in your own life?

_____

_____

_____

_____

_____

Notes:

_____
_____
_____
_____
_____
_____
_____
_____
_____
_____
_____
_____
_____
_____
_____
_____
_____
_____
_____
_____
_____
_____
_____
_____
_____
_____

"When I stand before God at the end of my life, I would hope that I would not have a single bit of talent left, and could say, 'I used everything you gave me.'"

—Erma Bombeck

6 YOUR T-N-T

Please reference Chapter 7 in the book, Your Divine Fingerprint and Session 6 of the DVD teaching series.

TRANSACTIONAL VERSUS TRANSFORMATIONAL
Your call to live with a transcendent purpose!

Transformation: Webster's 1828 Dictionary defines transformation as metamorphosis. It goes on to define metamorphosis...

> *"Metamorphosis: as from a caterpillar to a butterfly; a change of heart in man by which his disposition and temper are conformed to the divine image."*

Change is a constant. It's all around us all the time. Change happens whether we want it to or not, whether we like it or not, whether we acknowledge it or not, whether we see ourselves as a part of the change or not. The fact is, things are going to change. We will always be in the midst of some kind of metamorphosis.

List some changes in life you are currently experiencing.

_____

_____

_____

_____

_____

Although things are going to change, that doesn't always mean they are going to change for the better. With all change that happens to us and around us, we get the opportunity to choose how we let it affect us. The truth is that WE are the ones who decide if things change for the better. Once we reconcile in our minds that change is real, change is constant, and that we can't opt out, we can choose to make sure that we are engaged in the change so that our changes become changes for the better.

> "It's not what happens to you that matters most but what happens in you which ultimately determines what happens through you."
>
> —Your Divine Fingerprint, p.121

Most of us get stuck at some point in our lives because of what has happened to us in the past and we are unable to move forward. We don't realize that we have the power, regardless of what happens to us, to let what happens mature us (digest, discern and learn the lessons). When we learn the lessons and mature, God is able to do in us what He needs to do for our growth and our good.

Romans 8:28 (NKJV)
And we know that all things work together for good to those who love God, to those who are the called according to His purpose.

Most often, we get stuck in our past because we have not made a crucial transition in our thinking. As children we experience life in a very transactional manner. We do something well or master some new skill and there are positive rewards, appreciation, or celebration. It is stimulus and response, action and consequence, exchange of like for like. For children this is appropriate and beneficial but as they mature and grow they are supposed to out-grow this transactional, reactionary mindset and begin living based on their core values and who they decide they want to be. Many normal thinking adults never make this crucial transition in mindset. They get stuck in the rut of transactional relationships. "You scratch my back, and I'll scratch yours." Actions, reactions and consequences are the norm of everyday life and shape their decision and relationships. The truth is that it's a HARD way to live. Hurt feelings, perceived rejections, and disappointments lead them to put less and less effort in their jobs, in their friendships, and in their families. They often find them-selves immersed in conflict as a result.

Most conflict happens when we don't "get" what we feel we deserve.

We may say to ourselves,

- "If they're not going to do that, I'm not going to do it either."

- "If they don't pay me extra for going above and beyond then I won't."

- "The last time I bought her flowers she didn't respond the way I hoped so I won't do THAT anymore."

We do what we do based on what someone else does or doesn't do. This is how most people live their lives.

Describe a time in your own life where you have been on the transactional (reactionary) side of a relationship? What was the outcome?

_____

_____

_____

_____

_____

If to be transactional is to be reactionary, then the journey to be transformational begins when we stop reacting and start being proactive. When we choose to deploy our Divine Fingerprint and bring the best us that we can be into every situation, regardless of a person's behavior toward us, we get to experience Transformational living.

Transformational Leadership then, supersedes stimulus and response. The essence of being Transformational is to live on the proactive side of life. When you choose to operate with a Transformational Leadership mindset, you strategically choose your response to someone's behavior towards you based on what is best, based on your core values and based on what YOU bring to the relationship, NOT what they did or didn't do.

Revisit your answer to the question above. In this situation, how could you have been more proactive instead of reactive?

_____

_____

_____

THE ONE THING

Read Luke 10:38-42, John 12:1-8

In this story, was Martha living on the transactional or transformational side of life? _____

In the moment she was caught up with the concerns of her task and missed the opportunity to focus on the gift of being at Jesus's feet. Later in scripture the same thing happened with Judas. He was caught up with concerns about how much the perfume cost that Mary used to anoint the feet of Jesus rather than honoring Jesus and putting Him first.

In Luke 10:42, and John 12:8; God's Word says that Jesus is meant to be the focal point. Both Martha and Judas lost sight of what was most important. Instead of focusing on what truly mattered most they were distracted by things that seemed important in the moment. When we become task focused we move into a TRANSACTIONAL mindset. Transformational thinking focuses on the larger picture and values relationships over tasks.

We've all heard the common wisdom about keeping the "main thing" the main thing. In reality, we need to make Jesus our ONE THING, our only thing!

The proof of your transformation is what you decide to put first!

How can we prevent urgent tasks (tasks of the moment) from distracting us from the ONLY thing in our lives?

_____

_____

_____

What can you do today to reorder your life and focus more on the one thing that matters most in every area?

_____

_____

_____

What keeps you from focusing on the one thing? Most people "follow their heart." They don't ever realize that the heart is meant to be a follower, not a leader. _"Where your treasure is, there your heart will be also."_ - Matthew 6:21

We need to have the same response to Jesus that Mary did. When we get the opportunity, acknowledge Him as being first in our lives and see past the task to live with a transcendent cause.

Read John 11:1-45

Again, Martha has an interesting response to Jesus. She is seemingly more concerned with the smell of Lazarus than she is with the power of Jesus. If we are not intentional about our thinking and prioritize the value of who Jesus is and His power in our lives, we can have the same response as Martha. We can be more concerned with how our "stuff" appears than with what Jesus wants to do in the midst of our "stuff".

Jesus isn't asking us to raise anything from the dead in our own strength, we just have to be willing to remove the stone blocking Jesus from doing what He wants to do. Normal (Transactional) thinking finds excuses for why the stone can't be rolled away, Transformational thinking heeds Jesus's voice asking us to roll the stone away from what He wants most to heal.

What are some stones that you need to move out of the way in your life?

_____

_____

_____

In reality, Martha's heart was to serve. The problem was that she didn't lead her heart to focus on what mattered most in that moment. She was more focused on the task than on Jesus's presence. So how do we focus on the One Thing, make our things about Him, and roll the stones away in our life to let Jesus heal what needs to be healed? The answer is found in our everyday life. How we bring our best to our work, raise our families, handle our relationships, serve others, etc... this is where the evidence of our transformation is found and it is in all these things that we bring honor to God by operating in our 1% and doing ALL things as unto Him. Ultimately, your fingerprint isn't really even about you, it's about what God wants to do in the earth through you and the 1% He has given you. Our responsibility many times is to get out of the way and let God do His thing. To God, the thing is never about the thing, but everything is about everything. When we make our "things" about Him, He knows that He can do amazing things through us as a result of our willingness to obey.

Sacrifice Short-Term Rewards for the Benefits of Long-Term Vision

Mary poured a box of ointment on Jesus that was equivalent to a year's wages for the average worker. She was willing to give up this treasure because of her love for Jesus.

> "Reward says 'What will I get if I do this?' and is based on what has been and what is. Vision says, 'I will give my best' and is based on what is possible"
>
> —Your Divine Fingerprint, p.130

Mary gave her best, she gave her all to the Lord she loved. We should do no less! When we give less than our best to Jesus, we have made no sacrifice at all.

It is not until we give our all that we are truly displaying our love for Him. When we shortchange Jesus with our time, our tithes, and our talents, we are not displaying our love for Him. He wants the very best FROM you so He can do HIS very best IN you!

What does it mean to you to give your very best to God?

_____

_____

_____

_____

_____

How can you give your very best to others (your family, friends, co-workers)?

_____

_____

_____

_____

_____

Overcome Your Objectives... To Create an Unstoppable Culture

Mary took her focus off of what she personally wanted to accomplish, and instead, she made her life about what God wanted to create in and around her... In other words, "She gave up everything she herself desired and in turn received everything her soul desired."

Objectives and goals are important, but we have to be willing to sacrifice what we want for what we know is most important.

What are some short-term goals or objectives that you have right now? Are you willing to sacrifice those temporarily to put God first?

_____

_____

_____

Step back from these goals and objectives and observe them.

How can you be better about putting God first?

_____

_____

_____

_____

_____

When we put God first, God takes what we have and makes it unstoppable. He is the kind of God that is able to do "immeasurably more than you can ask, or imagine." (Ephesians 3:20)

DEPLOYING YOUR TRANSFORMATION

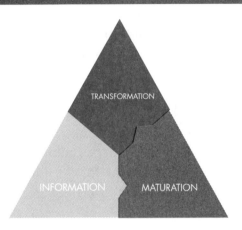

DISCOVER INFORMATION

All of us are given information. Information by itself does nothing for us. We may have received this information in school or at our job.

The first lesson of becoming transformational is learning to value information. No one can ever determine for you what you are going to learn. So learn from everything! Remember these three things about learning:

1. **Your life lessons are your life lessons**
   You decide what experiences you learn from, good and bad.

2. **Learn from the mistakes of others**

Make a choice to learn from the man next to the bridge with tattered clothing holding a sign that says "the bridge is out." You don't have to experience everything for yourself. Nor do you want to!

3. **What you learn is what you EARN.**
When we decide to take the information presented to us and assimilate it, we build more earning power for the future because we gain the ability to be competent like we haven't before.

Ask yourself these questions:

What are three areas of your life where you can move from transactional to transformational?

_____

_____

_____

_____

What experience have you had that you can go back and learn new lessons from?

_____

_____

_____

_____

What are three ways you can learn from the mistakes of others?

_____

_____

_____

_____

_____

Develop a learning agenda.
Simply sit down and write some things you want to learn. And go learn them!

_____

_____

_____

_____

DEVELOP MATURATION

Maturation is happening for you right now! The word maturation means "the emergence of personal and behavioral competencies through growth."

The road to empowerment is to take the information you have been given and define to yourself what makes that information valuable. The key question is "how can I make the information I know work to my benefit?" Age does not signify maturity.

Maturity is the choice to actively take what you know and apply it in such a way as it produces positive results.

The worst enemy you will ever have is a byproduct of your immaturity: insecurity. In order to fight insecurity, one of the greatest things we can do is be willing to sacrifice something in the present for something better.

The Craft Family mission statement is: "Never allow the good to be the robber of the best." What is your mission statement?

_____

_____

_____

_____

_____

_____

Where do you need to mature? List three things.

_____

_____

_____

_____

_____

_____

DEPLOY TRANSFORMATION

The way you live your life is largely determined by how you see yourself. Increasing your confidence requires that you become change focused in your life.

Don't just let change happen, be a change-agent. If something isn't working, change it for the better. If a relationship isn't working, don't walk away. Look at how you need to mature in the context of that relationship and transform it into something that is working.

Take the information that you know, and the information that you're learning and allow it to mature you and grow you into a better person than you were yesterday. This is the foundation to living as a transformational leader!

How can you deploy your mission statement and learning agenda to move from transactional to transformational in the three areas you need to mature?

_____

_____

_____

_____

_____

_____

"What we do repeatedly consciously becomes a subconscious force for better or for worse and is called habit-force."

—Leadershipology

7 YOUR HABIT FORCE

Please reference Chapter 8-9 in the book, Your Divine Fingerprint and Session 7 of the DVD teaching series.

Often, we discount the value of our words and our perceptions as well as the impact that our words and perceptions have on our beliefs, behaviors, and ultimately the good or bad things we experience in life. Under valuing our words and perceptions (especially of ourselves) is one of the most costly mistakes we can make. In reality, the words we speak and accept as fact about ourselves are incredibly powerful. Our words (and the words we accept as true about us) direct our thoughts, our thoughts (how we think) direct the choices we make, the choices we make over time become our habits and cement our character. Our choices, habits, and character are what drive our experiences which then become our life lessons. If we capture this process and harness it for our growth, advancement, and good, our outcome and what we eventually have in life will be order and prosperity. If we don't intentionally lead this process and allow negative words and perceptions on the front end, the result on the back end will be crisis and chaos.

Our life sentences — the sum of what we say in and over our life — literally "sentence" our life.

───── **YOUR WORDS DEFINE YOUR LIFE** ─────

Life comes in Words...
Words become Sentences...

Sentences become Messages...
Messages become Experiences...
Experiences become Life Lessons...
Just because you have gone through a pleth-
ora of life experiences does not qualify you to
be Experienced.
If you do not learn from your Experiences...
You will create a culture of Crisis...
Crisis in any area of our lives is a
second opportunity to learn a Life Lesson...
If you do not learn from your crisis experi-
ences in life...
You will Experience Chaos. The bad news
about Chaos is...
It leads to poverty.
If you choose to learn from your Experiences
You will create a culture of opportunities...
You will experience Order.
The good news about order is...
It leads to Prosperity.

—Keith Craft

Your words reflect your identity.
"For as he thinks in his heart, so is he." Proverbs 23:7a

Your words influence your thinking.
Your life sentences are the limiting beliefs that you accept about yourself that often times aren't true. We tend to hear negative statements about us and we adopt them as fact. If we intentionally choose to address these limiting

beliefs, we can begin to see ourselves as who we really are, who God says we are, and live life on another level!

What are some limiting beliefs that you have accepted about yourself and are holding you back?
(Example; "I'm just not as smart as other people." "I'm really not very pretty." "I'm just socially awkward." "I'm really not very likable.")

_____

_____

_____

_____

In what ways have these limiting beliefs have held you back?
(Example; Chances you didn't take, relationships you walked away from, businesses you chose not to start or try.)

_____

_____

_____

Your words can change your world.
Your words and the "facts" you accept about yourself either imprison you or LIBERATE you!

Resentence your life!
Life comes in words.
    Believe.

<u>Words become sentences.</u>
Believe in God.
Believe in yourself.
Believe in others.

<u>Sentences become messages.</u>
It is impossible to practice Think, Be, Do in a way that is inconsistent with what you believe about yourself.

<u>Messages become our experiences.</u>
What you believe will determine what you achieve.

<u>Our experiences become our life lessons:</u>
Lesson 1: The proof of what you believe will be evidenced by how you Think, Be, Do life.

Lesson2: People will not believe in you if you don't believe in yourself.

Lesson 3: You will not believe in yourself if you do not live what you believe to be true.

Lesson 4: For you to achieve anything great, you must align your life with people who believe in you.

Deploy your new words and new life sentences to create new life lessons in your life. If you catch yourself making a negative life sentence, stop, correct, apologize, and restate it as a new life sentence. Ask for assistance. Recognize that this is a lifelong process.

YOUR HABIT FORCE

What we consciously repeat becomes a subcounscious force — for better or for worse — a habit-force.

The Power of Habit

I am your constant companion.
I am your greatest helper or your heaviest burden.
I will push you onward or drag you down to failure.
I am completely at your command.
Half the things you do, you might just as well turn over to me,
And I will be able to do them quickly and correctly.
I am easily managed; you must merely be firm with me.
Show me exactly how you want something done,
And after a few lessons I will do it automatically.
I am the servant of all great men,
And, alas, of all failures as well.
Those who are great, I have made great.
Those who are failures, I have made failures.
I am not a machine, though I work with all the precision of a machine,
Plus, the intelligence of a man.
You may run me for profit, or run me for ruin;
It makes no difference to me.
Take me, train me, be firm with me
And I will put the world at your feet.
Be easy with me, and I will destroy you.
Who am I?
I am HABIT!

We are creatures of Habit

In the 1828 Webster's Dictionary, habit is defined as:

> *1. A coat worn by ladies over other garments. State of any thing; implying some continuance or permanence; temperament or particular state of a body, formed by nature or induced by extraneous circumstances; as a costive or lax habit of body; a sanguine habit.*

Our habits are things we can put on or take off!

> *2. A disposition or condition of the mind or body acquired by custom or a frequent repetition of the same act. Habit is that which is held or retained, the effect of custom or frequent repetition. Hence we speak of good habits and bad habits.*

Fundamentally, habits are things we acquire. Our habits start as routines, or even things that we like. As we do these things more, the less we start ruling them and the more they start ruling us. A habit is something that we create, either strategically or by default in our life. Your habits can force you into a place of success or failure within your life. Our habits are things that we decide, but ultimately they can end up deciding for us. They can be one of our greatest forces of success, or they can be one of our greatest forces of failure.

What are some of the habits, either for the positive or for the negative, you have formed over the course of your

life? List any you can think of.

_____

_____

_____

How have these habits contributed to your failure or success?

_____

_____

_____

_____

_____

——————— HABIT FORCE FACTS ———————

Habit is a principle given to us by God.

Habit is a principle that is given to us by God. It's meant to develop an instinctive nature of repetition to do right things to the point where doing what God wants us to do is automatic. Your habits comprise vital elements of your 1%. This is true because your character is not built on what you INTEND to do, but rather on what you actually do. Therefore when you choose to utilize the gift God has given you, your Habit Force, to shape your DOing, you begin the process of becoming the person you most want to be.

Habits evidence the true desire of our hearts.

Many times our habits arise out of a desire to please ourselves. We lead ourselves to a place where what we want not only determines what we do, but it can begin to control what we do. Are we making the choices today that become habits tomorrow based on comfort, temporary pleasure, or becoming all that God has made us to be?

No one picks up their first drink of liquor with a desire to become an alcoholic. A habit is formed when a person who is an alcoholic no longer is in control.

DISCOVER YOUR WINNING EDGE – YOUR 1%!

In a 10 year span, the average margin of victory at the Daytona 500 has been 1.54 seconds.

1st Place: $1,278,813

2nd Place: $621,321

The 1 second difference = $657,492.

The margin of victory at the 2012 Olympic Games between a Gold medal and no medal was infinitesimal:

Men's 100 Meter Results: 2012 Summer Olympics

1. Usain Bolt	9.63
2. Yohan Blake	9.75
3. Juston Gatlin	9.79

In 2008, Michael Phelps beat Milorad Cavic in the 100m butterfly by .01. One hundredth of a second to earn his seventh gold medal.

We don't often think of the power of a second, but a second, or even a hundredth of a second, has the power to change everything.

Read John 4:1-26

No one can tell you what to practice, but you must know in your life what you need to practice so that your passion for anything can grow. The more you practice, the greater your passion for what you practice grows. When you practice your passion, you develop the power to see a vision for what you want in life.

PRACTICE DOING WHAT YOU NEED TO DO

"Practicing is a critical component of the Discovering and Developing process to elevating your greatness. Practicing allows you to discover your gifts, talents, and attributes so you can focus on and Develop the areas of your life that elevate your passion, create your purpose to excel, generate a drive within you, and make you unstoppable... practice is the secret of the instinctive greatness of your 1%."

- Your Divine Fingerprint, p. 181

Where in life do you feel like your passion is lacking? How can you practice better to build your passion?

_____

_____

_____

_____

Name at least one thing that you are passionate about that has the power to develop a vision for you.

_____

_____

_____

When you practice forgiveness, you have the power to no longer be offended.

When you practice gratitude, you produce a positive attitude. Gratefulness is the antidote for negativity.

When you practice giving your best, you bring excellence wherever you go.

Your best, the best that God has given you, is directly tied to your fingerprint. The imprint that you leave is whatever you practice with other people.

Practice bringing your greatness into every sphere! Bringing your greatness is NOT contingent upon whether or not it will be reciprocated, it's not contingent upon how much you are or are not being paid, it's not even contingent upon whether or not your greatness is even noticed! In the end, part of our reward is who we are becoming as a result of choosing to PRACTICE GREATNESS! Additionally we can rest in the fact that God our Father is a rewarder of things done in secret (even if no one else notices)! Focusing on what you are getting back from a person, an employer, or a situation is the devil's goal. It puts you to be in a position in life where you only give as good as you get.

What do you need to start practicing today?

_____

_____

_____

When you choose to practice, it develops your instinctive greatness. Whatever you choose to practice makes you better not just at that one thing, it has the power to develop your habit to have excellence in everything.

Be Willing to Give People A Drink of What You Have

In John 4:39-42 when Jesus asked the Samaritan woman for a drink, she didn't immediately give it to Him, she had to process. We can be the same. We think about the last time someone placed a demand on us, how we were hurt before. We start to think about all the reasons why we shouldn't give someone a drink: our hurt, our disillusionment, our issues. Look at Jesus in this story. Jesus was not truly focused on what the Samaritan woman could do for him. He was focused on what He could give her.

We have all experienced relationships that haven't worked out, and we're often wounded as a result. Most people walk away from these relationships and say to themselves, "I'll never let anyone hurt me like that again." This causes them to withhold their greatness from any relationship because of their fear that it will not work out. Even in the midst of our relationships we have the power to practice.

List some times in your life where you've allowed past pain to determine what you give to something current.

_____

_____

_____

_____

The Samaritan woman didn't come to the well just thirsty; she came to the well wounded, broken, and battered. Jesus showed up at the well not just to give her water; but to show her that often times our way – the human way, ends in brokenness. But Jesus wants us to try life His way and drink what He has to offer so that we can pour out whatever He has given us to others.

In order to choose to give a person something to drink, you have to make the decision to be an energy producer. If you're a parent or an employer you may know what it is like to have people around you that demand your attention and energy all the time. Think of your favorite people in your life. These are most likely the people who are energy producers for you. We are energy producers for others when we give people a drink of what we have. As an energy producer, we are not focused on the value they add to us, we are focused on the value that we add to them.

This is what Jesus is trying to show us through this story. Your responsibility is to transition at some point in your life from demanding energy from people, to producing energy for them.

What are some ways that you can sometimes be energy demanding?

_____

_____

_____

Based on your 1%, how can you produce energy in other's lives?

_____

_____

_____

One of the best ways to get past the pain of your past and give someone your best is to look at what happened in your past as practice for your future. It doesn't matter what someone did or didn't do to you, it was meant to be practice to make you better in the future.

The habit force that you have is either going to force you to win or force you to lose. To get where God wants you to be, you have to begin to take ownership of the 1% He has given you. Take your habits and shape them, don't let them shape you.

God has put something in you that needs to be developed. And when you choose to develop yourself, you can give people the best part of you; which is really the best part of God. When you PRACTICE the greatness God put in you, you develop the power to make miracles happen!

DEVELOP YOUR LIFE SENTENCES

Your life sentences sentence your life. Whatever you decide to say about yourself will become the punishment or blessing that you sentence yourself to. The words you choose define your life. You can say whatever you want to say about yourself but it isn't until you begin to say what God says about you that the sentence of your life can change. A life sentence is anything that you consistently speak over yourself.

We can often think that because we have had experiences, we are experienced. Having an experience doesn't make you experienced. You can probably think of someone right now, it may even be yourself, who has grown older and has had experiences, but has not gotten any better. They have experienced life but their life has not caused them to grow or develop.

Here are some life sentences you may have heard/said and next to them are what God wants you to say:

- "I'll never amount to anything." – "I am who God says I am!"
- "I can't win for losing" – "God made me to win!"
- "I'll believe it when I see it." – "All things are possible with God!"

Newton's 2nd Law of Thermodynamics introduces the concept of entropy. Entropy is the loss of energy and order in any system caused by the lack of force being added to the system. In essence, a top eventually stops spinning and falls over, cars in neutral lose speed and come to a stop, and beautiful gardens eventually are overgrown by weeds and lose their beauty. It's the same principle that drives your habit force. If we don't begin to intentionally choose to say the right things and believe the right things about ourselves, then we can reasonably expect that over time we will lose momentum, order, and prosperity and be left to accept stagnation, disarray, and poverty. We must choose to add the necessary energy to say the right things, believe the right things, and make our choices accordingly, if we want to overcome entropy and use this process for our development, so we can be empowered with the greatness of God made manifest in us through our 1% difference that becomes our 1% power.

What is a life sentence you have had that you feel has sentenced your life?

_____

_____

_____

There are three main ways to learn a life lesson:

1. Experience

2. Crisis

3. Chaos

If you choose not to learn from your experiences, you will create a culture of crisis around you. Crisis in any area of our lives is the second opportunity to learn a life lesson. When we choose not to learn from what we experience, we force ourselves to experience difficulty.

Are there any crisis points in your life today? Have you experienced crisis or even chaos in your past? What can you learn from that situation that you can begin to practice differently to ensure you don't have to revisit/ relive that crisis?

_____

_____

_____

_____

_____

_____

_____

_____

If you choose not to learn from your crisis, you open up the door for chaos in your life. The bad news is that chaos leads to poverty. Not just financial poverty. When you have chaos in your life, you open the door for scarcity in any area. Financially, relationally, physically (your health) and anywhere else there is chaos.

Chaos is the third, and worst way to have to learn a lesson. It is the very definition of learning a lesson through the pain of losing something.

However, both chaos and crisis can be avoided if you choose to learn from your experiences. If you choose to learn from an experience, you create an opportunity in whatever areas you choose to learn in. When you can seize opportunities effectively you have the power to create prosperity financially, relationally, physically, and everywhere else you seize an opportunity.

Our life sentences have the power to sentence our life experiences from crisis, to chaos, to poverty. But they also have the power to sentence our life experiences from opportunity, to order, to prosperity.

DEPLOYING YOUR HABIT FORCE

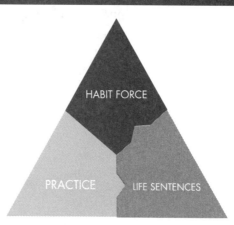

DISCOVER WHAT YOU NEED TO PRACTICE

You must begin to see the things that you need to practice in your life. You can't develop a habit without first knowing what kind of habit you are supposed to develop. To become aware of what you need to practice, ask yourself these questions.

What are you currently practicing in your life? Good or bad.

_____

_____

_____

_____

_____

_____

In what ways are you practicing to develop a positive habit force in one, or a few areas of your life? (marriage, job, business, relationships, etc.)

_____

_____

_____

_____

What do you do, naturally or on purpose that produces energy in these areas?

_____

_____

_____

_____

DEVELOP YOUR LIFE SENTENCES

Read: How to Win at Life on pages 181-185 in _Your Divine Fingerprint_

After reading the five things to practice everyday, what do you need to practice more to develop positive life sentences in these five areas?

_____

_____

_____

How can you start being more of an energy producer today?

_____

_____

_____

_____

_____

_____

DEPLOY YOUR HABIT FORCE

Whatever you decide to practice awakens the potential of your 1%. As you begin to discover your ability to practice the right thing, you will develop positive life sentences. As you begin to develop positive life sentences, you will deploy the right kind of habits in your life. These habits will awaken your 1% like nothing has before.

What kind of habits do you think your practice is going to develop in your life?

_____

_____

_____

_____

_____

_____

What kind of results do you anticipate your positive life sentences are going to produce?

_____

_____

_____

_____

_____

_____

Notes:

_____

_____

_____

_____

_____

_____

_____

_____

_____

_____

_____

_____

_____

_____

_____

_____

_____

_____

"Your 1% Power is not intended to be displayed only once...It is who you are and who God made you to be. Remember, your 1% has the power it has for one simple reason - God!"

—*Your Divine Fingerprint, p. 249*

8 YOUR UNSTOPPABLE FORCE

Please reference Chapter 10-12 in the book, Your Divine Fingerprint and Session 8 of the DVD teaching series.

You are an unstoppable force! As the pieces of your 1% come together, you will see that your divine fingerprint (your, "Christ in me and I in Christ") is what gives you the power to operate in your genius capacity and to be an unstoppable force! Get ready! If you'll learn and apply the material in this chapter, your world will work like never before!

─────── **DISCOVER WHO JESUS REALLY IS** ───────

In Matthew chapter 16 Jesus asks His disciples, *"Who do people say that the Son of Man is?"* He already knew the answer but He was asking the question with a purpose. He was leading their thinking. They answered, *"Some say John the Baptist, some say Elijah, and others say Jeremiah or one of the other prophets."* Jesus followed up with another question, *"But who do YOU say I am?"* (emphasis added) Jesus is asking much more than a question here, He is asking them to come to a conclusion. Jesus walked and talked with His disciples daily. He taught them directly and they had a front row seat for all of the miracles. Jesus is so much more than just a great teacher or a guy that could do miracles.

The first step to becoming an unstoppable force is having a clear revelation of who God is.

Peter pipes up with, "*You are the Christ, the Son of the living God.*" Jesus answers Peter, "*Blessed are you, Simon son of Jonah, for this was not revealed to you by flesh and blood, but by my Father in heaven. And I tell you that you are Peter and on this rock I will build my church, and the gates of Hell will not overcome it.*" Because Jesus is the Christ, He had the power to make the impossible possible and He still has that power today!

The distinction Jesus was looking for in these questions is the difference between knowing Him as a teacher, miracle worker, and healer or coming to the understanding that He is so much more than miracles and teaching. Best of all, He wants to be in relationship with us personally. Have you decided to stop knowing ABOUT Jesus and start KNOWING Him as your savior, redeemer, and friend? It's His power IN us that makes us UNSTOPPABLE!

The greatest question that Jesus continues to ask to this day is the same question He asked two thousand years ago. "*Who do YOU say I am?*"

Read Matthew 18:1-4

To truly understand who Jesus is, you have to decide to become like a little child.

In this passage the disciples ask Jesus who the greatest in His kingdom is. He says that unless you change your mind to that of a little child, you cannot enter the Kingdom of Heaven. If you are going to have a true revelation of who Jesus is, you have to make the decision to humble yourself and say, "I believe."

Your ability to be unstoppable is directly related to your belief in who Jesus is.

Who is Jesus to you?

_____

_____

_____

DEVELOP WHO YOU REALLY ARE

Becoming an unstoppable force is not predicated on your natural gifts and talents. It's not about your desire to personally grow and develop, or your belief. Becoming an unstoppable force begins and ends with your understanding of who you really are.

God created you with a fingerprint that is distinctive. It is yours alone. It was one of the first things to develop before you were born and it will be one of the last things to deteriorate when you pass on. There is a natural/supernatural correlation there. Until recently, fingerprints have really only been used to identify a person at the scene of a crime, but it paints a picture of your 1% difference that allows you to leave an imprint no one else can leave.

Your understanding of who you really are will help you to comprehend the power of your imprint on the world. You will leave an imprint wherever you go because you still have a fingerprint regardless if you understand what it symbolizes or not, but you may never understand the power of that imprint if you do not understand who you really are.

- **What imprints have you left on people or situations in your life? Good and Bad.**

_____

_____

_____

Identify and Deal With Your Blind Spots

The way to become aware and develop who you really are is to remove your blind spots.

Your blind spots can be anything in your life that keeps you from being successful.

> "Blind Spots are the parts of you that you don't see that are keeping you from being all that you can be."
>
> – Your Divine Fingerprint, p.195

In life, blind spots are often obvious to others, but we're oblivious to them... Blind spots are the parts of our paradigm that we think are perfectly acceptable, yet our actions do not produce energy in others and it causes more harm than good... Blind spots are the things that we consider to be truthful, but are actually truth-fool because we bought into something that's not actually true, it's just what we believe to be true... Blind spots are invisible areas of our lives that build invisible walls around us and cause visible success or outcomes to elude us... Blind spots are the delusions born out of a desire to live with minimal pain and discomfort.

God puts people in your life to make you aware of your blind spots. These people are not in your life to wound you, they are placed in your life by God to make you aware of where you need to grow. God gives these people to you as gifts. They enable you to sidestep pitfalls and not allow yourself to be stopped by the things you didn't even know would stop you. Your wife, husband, children, boss, friends and other people are in your life to expose your blind spots, so that you can become unstoppable!

You must know yourself and be willing to remove blind spots in your life if you are going to become unstoppable. The alignments you have in your life are there to help you grow. Many people go through life with the same alignments, or seeking alignments that will not challenge them because of their search for comfort and minimal pain.

If you are going to be an unstoppable force, you have to allow the way that you are today to be challenged, so that you can become the person God has created you to be tomorrow.

What alignments has God put in your life to enable you to identify and deal with your blind spots?

_____

_____

_____

_____

_____

_____

_____

What blind spots do you need to address today so that you can become an unstoppable force?

_____

_____

_____

_____

———— EMBRACE RESISTANCE! ————

Average or "normal" thinking people view resistance as a steering mechanism. "Well that's difficult so I'll just do something else." "Weightlifting is hard, it's just not for me." They avoid resistance wherever they can so instead of embracing resistance, they resist resistance. Typically this is an effort to minimize discomfort and avoid pain. The truth is that we will all have to deal with pain and discomfort in life, but if we can embrace resistance today we will be ready for difficulties when they arise. Just think of it, if you knew you were going to have to run a marathon one year from today, you'd begin training (if you were wise). You wouldn't put it off because it will make the experience ahead of you manageable and just maybe even enjoyable! If you put the training off because it's uncomfortable, how miserable will you be when the big day comes?

God wants the things that are uncomfortable or painful for you to actually cause you to grow and make you stronger. This thought process can be summed up simply, "Do easy things = have a hard life. Do hard things = enjoy an easy life." It may seem counter intuitive, but it's absolutely true. Embrace resistance in your life today and see great results in your future!

What areas in your life can you identify opportunities to embrace what resists you? How will this set you up for success in the future and make you unstoppable?

_____

_____

_____

_____

Identify and Develop Your Genius

> *"Genius: a particular nature, disposition, aptitude, or character that directs one's course of life"*
> *– Webster's 1828 Dictionary*

"Genius means little more than the faculty of perceiving in an un-habitual way."
- William James

———— **DEPLOY YOUR 1% POWER** ————

In short, a genius is someone who can solve a problem that others can't. They know what to do, how to do it, when to do it, why they need to do it, and, because they are willing to do it, they are a GENIUS!

A defining characteristic of a Genius is that they know how to BENEFIT from problems that bring others to a standstill.

I am Your Problem

I am a Reality in your everyday.
I have many names, many faces, many shapes
and I come in every size and color.
I am blamed for more failures than anything or
anyone else.
I am no respecter of persons. I do not play favor-
ites and I never choose sides.
Within me are invisible seeds of greatness and
immeasurable fields of frustration. What you
choose to do with me will make you better or
make you bitter.
The people who don't want me the most, inev-
itably have the most of me. The great paradox
is that I will never go away, but yet I can show
anyone a better way.
Without me there would be zero success! In fact,
I am the driving force behind all achievement
and the better you get at dealing with me, the
better you...you will be.
It's not a matter of IF you will face me, but
WHEN you will face me...and with that, let me
make you a guarantee...I will be in your face
every day.
I am the one thing in your life that has the poten-
tial to help you Think Bigger...Be better...and Do
the Impossible in every area of your life.
Unfortunately, until you meet me, everything is
fine and like most people say, "It is what it is!"
Those people by the way, don't know the power I
have to make their potential a reality.
The most important thing about me that you need
to know is...I am waiting everyday to be used

by you or in worst case scenarios, to be used
against you.
Who am I?
I am Your Problem and in case no one has told
you...my last name is Solution!
- Keith A. Craft

Each of us has the innate potential for God given genius and it can be expressed through us in as many unusual and unique ways as can be imagined.

There are four core things that geniuses do to become great problem solvers:

1. Geniuses identify THE problem. (the real or root problem)

2. Geniuses A-A-P everything.
   - Assess
   - Address
   - Progress

3. Geniuses define the problem.

4. Geniuses benefit from the problem.

There's more than one kind of genius! Two simple examples of this are technical problem solvers and relational problem solvers.

Technical problem solvers look at complex systems and readily comprehend how things work and where problems may arise. They are able to make the complicated seem simple in their minds and know how to solve problems that would confound others. Some people look at car engines and think, "That's straight forward." (That's amazing!!!) Others, like me, look at an engine and think, "I'd better call a mechanic right away!"

Relational problem solvers look at interactions between people and readily comprehend what the individual parties need, and understand motives/expectations. These people are characterized by friends that often ask for relationship advice. They hear things like, "You always know just what to say."

What area can you identify in your life that God made you GREAT at?

_____

_____

_____

_____

_____

Are you a technical problem solver? Relational? Neither? Maybe you have another innate ability to solve problems. The fact is that you DO have a sweet spot! God HAS empowered you! If you only focus on areas where you struggle you may never comprehend the GREATNESS that God has put in you!

"Everybody is a genius. But if you judge a fish by its ability to climb a tree, it will live its whole life believing it is stupid."
– Albert Einstein

You were created by God with the capacity for genius, to solve problems that others couldn't. When you solve problems, you add value to your life and to the lives around you. The more problems you solve for someone, the more value you add to their life. Many people do not see themselves as a solution to another person's problem. Don't sell yourself (and God) short. When we play small and fail to be a problem solver we actually become a part of the problem.

<u>Focus on the imprint YOU were made to leave!</u>

Often we allow hurts and hang ups from our past to disempower us from deploying our 1% and leaving the imprint we were made for. We focus on the negative imprint someone left on our lives or the lack of imprint from someone we should have been able to count on. Blame and unforgiveness shackle the greatness God put in us and problems are left unresolved.

First, when we operate within unforgiveness and blame we are the ones that are bound. Often the person at the root of our resentments is unaware and unaffected.

Second, and most importantly, the call of God on your life isn't conditional or dependent on the actions or behaviors of another. You have to run YOUR race. Don't get side tracked by how well (or not well) someone else is doing in THEIR race. YOUR race is your race and your imprint is YOUR imprint! Don't ever hold back the good you can do based on the bad that someone else has done. God is still counting on you to do what only you can do with the one of a kind fingerprint He gave you!

Many people never end up deploying their 1% because they allow the negative imprint another person left keep them from revealing the genius that God gave them.

Are there unresolved issues in your life that you've allowed to hold you back from deploying your 1%? What will you do differently to bring your 1% without restraint going forward?

_____

_____

_____

_____

John 14:5-7 (NKJV)

[5] *Thomas said to him, "Lord, we don't know where you are going, so how can we know the way?"* [6] *Jesus answered, "I am the way and the truth and the life. No one comes to the Father except through me.* [7] *If you really know me, you will know my Father as well. From now on, you do know him and have seen him."*

To deploy your 1% you must have a true understanding of who Jesus is. The disciples didn't believe they knew the way. Jesus answered and said knowing Him is the same as knowing the way.

Knowing Jesus is the way to discover, develop, and then deploy your 1% power, your divine fingerprint, and your divine genius. It's the foundation to using your fingerprint to leave an imprint that no one else can leave. What you believe will ultimately become the way you behave. In order to truly deploy your 1% power, you have to believe what God says about you!

What DOES God says about you? What scripture can you find where God talks about the amazing creation He's made in you?

_____

_____

_____

John 14:12-14 (NKJV)
[12] Very truly I tell you, whoever believes in me will do the works I have been doing, and they will do even greater things than these, because I am going to the Father. [13] And I will do whatever you ask in my name, so that the Father may be glorified in the Son. [14] You may ask me for anything in my name, and I will do it.

According to Jesus, through Him you have the power within you to do greater works than He did in the earth! God wants to do great works THROUGH you so that He can be glorified IN you! If you can believe, God will use you as a living epistle of His grace, mercy, and power. You are the living proof that He is God and that He is good! God will use you to give HOPE to the people He brings across your path!

When you decide to put your trust fully in God, you have the power to become an unstoppable force. God has given you a fingerprint; a deposit of His glory. He gave you a fingerprint so that you could leave an imprint so that you will have the power to leave a deposit of God's glory on the earth that no one else can leave.

What do you need to trust God with right now?

_____

_____

_____

_____

_____

_____

How are you going to leave an imprint on the earth for God?

_____

_____

_____

_____

_____

_____

DEPLOYING YOUR UNSTOPPABLE FORCE

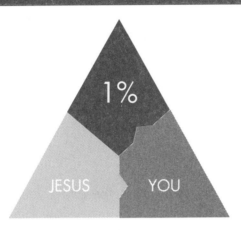

Look at your hand. Think of your entire life as your fingerprint. You are truly unique. You have greatness inside of you that no one else has. God gave you His glory unlike anyone else on earth!

DISCOVER WHO JESUS REALLY IS

To become an unstoppable force, you must realize that God is your creator. He wants to be the Lord and Savior of your life. He gave you His Son as a sacrifice, He offers you everlasting life, and the strength you need to accomplish anything and everything.

If you want to dedicate, or recommit your life to Jesus, it's simple. Just pray this prayer.

Dear Heavenly Father, I ask you to forgive me where I have missed the mark. I choose today to accept Jesus Christ as my Lord and Savior. Thank you, Father, for my uniqueness. Empower me today, Lord, to discover my 1% so that I can live a purposeful life. Help me today to live everyday with your power in my life. Amen"

It's that easy. As soon as you allow yourself to discover who Jesus really is you allow Him to show you who you are and who He has created you to be.

DEVELOP WHO YOU REALLY ARE

To develop who you really are, you must develop your relationship with God. You also must develop your relationships with people enough to become aware of your blind spots and change them.

What paradigms are you discovering you have that may be blind spots?

_____

_____

_____

_____

_____

_____

Ask a person that loves you what they think your blind spots are and list them here.

_____

_____

_____

_____

What is an ongoing strategy you can use to deal with your blind spots consistently?

_____

_____

_____

_____

DEPLOY YOUR 1% POWER

Through this study guide, you have learned to discover, develop and deploy the fingerprint that God has given you to leave an imprint on the world!

You are unstoppable! There is no reason to wait. Start today by taking the fingerprint, the greatness that God has given you and applying that to every relationship and situation you are in.

God has created you for greatness! He has given you a 1% that cannot be stopped because it comes from who He is. Make the decision today to become an unstoppable force!

What have you allowed to stop you and what are you going to begin to do today so that you are no longer stopped, but become an unstoppable force?

_____

_____

_____

_____

_____

_____

How can you begin to apply your 1% today?

_____

_____

_____

_____

_____

_____

_____

_____

_____

_____

_____

_____

Notes:

_____

_____

_____

_____

_____

_____

_____

_____

_____

_____

_____

_____

_____

_____

_____

_____

_____

_____

_____

_____

_____

_____

_____

_____

About the Author

Keith Craft is the founder and lead pastor of Elevate Life Church in Frisco, Texas. He speaks in the world's largest business/success seminars and has shared the stage with former world leaders such as Bill Clinton, George Bush, Mikhail Gorbachev, and Margaret Thatcher. For the past twenty years he has spoken alongside Super Bowl–winning coaches such as Mike Ditka, Don Shula, Mike Shanahan, and Tony Dungy; MVP quarterbacks such as Terry Bradshaw, Joe Montana, and Peyton Manning; and entertainers such as Jerry Lewis, Bill Cosby, and Goldie Hawn. As a leadership coach and strategist, Craft is also the founder of Leadershipology.com, an online quote service.

Elevate Life Church

ELC is a non-denominational church founded in January of 2000 with a focus on leadership. We are confident that ELC is more than just a place to go on the weekend to get good teaching, but it is a place where people are loved, by God and others, where people can develop beneficial lifelong relationships with people that seek to be great for God. Love is demonstrated by the example of our many wonderful servant-leaders, and the quality relationships they develop.

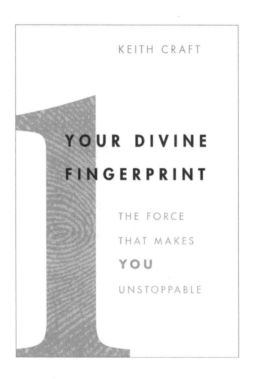

YOUR DIVINE FINGERPRINT

THE FORCE THAT MAKES **YOU** UNSTOPPABLE

by Keith Craft

www.keithcraft.org • 214-387-9833

Websites

Leadershipology.com

> Daily inspirational quotes to propel your leadership quest.

Leadershipshapers.com

> Purchase your annual membership and get on-board with a new, refreshing, leadership teaching by Keith Craft each month in your mailbox.

> Membership entitles you to additional discounts on Keith Craft's CD's and DVD's.

Keithcraft.org

> This is Keith Craft's blog where you can get inspiration on many topics such as, Leadership, Family, Faith, Business and more.

Other Books

Leadershipology 101

> The first in a series of 3 books containing Keith Craft's quotes (leadershipologies) and the thought behind each quote. This book is filled with tidbits of wisdom for every area of your life.